Kelly
of
Hazel Ridge

By Robbyn Smith van Frankenhuyzen
Illustrated by Gijsbert van Frankenhuyzen

For Kelly, our nature girl and the real writer in the family.

ACKNOWLEDGMENTS

First, we give a humongous thank-you to Kaitlyn Setter. By far, you were the easiest model we have ever worked with. Your eagerness to sit, stand, jump, walk, climb, smile, and crouch was amazing, and you did it all with smiles and laughs. You were an absolute joy to work with! Also thanks to Penny Setter, Kaitlyn's supportive mom, for your willingness to drive Kaitlyn to the farm so many times. And to Monica McCurdy and her mom Melissa, for spending a day at the Wildside Rehabilitation Center with us.

For their suggestions for a title for this book, our thanks also go to the students in the classrooms of Mrs. Bain, Mrs. Fuller, Mrs. Derksen and Mrs. Knapp.

Thanks to Theresa Moran for organizing a last-minute bullfrog hunt, and to Don Cowell and his hard-working draft horses. And finally, we thank Louise Sagaert (again) and all the volunteers at the Wildside Rehabilitation and Education Center in Eaton Rapids, Michigan, for your selfless devotion to all the injured and orphaned animals. Special gratitude to Darlene, who spent so much of her time with us. We know the Center survives on donations and volunteers. We appreciate everything you do.

Sleeping Bear Press™
310 North Main Street, Suite 300
Chelsea, MI 48118
www.sleepingbearpress.com

© 2006 Thomson Gale, a part of the Thomson Corporation.

Thomson, Star Logo and Sleeping Bear Press are trademarks and Gale is a registered trademark used herein under license.

Printed and bound in Canada

10 9 8 7 6 5 4 3 2 1

Library of Congress Cataloging-in-Publication Data on file.

⸎ INTRODUCTION ⸎

Hazel Ridge Farm was established as a family farm in rural Bath, Michigan, in the early 1900s. Tom Robson and his family built the farmhouse first and then the barn in 1914. It remained in the Robson family until the early 1940s when it was bought by one of the many Hart families residing in the area.

In 1980, a flyer advertising a "farm with 10 acres" came in the mail. Gijsbert and I loved the place so much we purchased it and were even married in the backyard with all our friends and family present. Here at Hazel Ridge we have raised our two daughters, Heather and Kelly, and it is here we hope to live out the rest of our days. For us it is a place of refuge that revives the tired soul.

—*Enjoy,*
Robbyn and Gijsbert
(a.k.a. Mr. Nick)

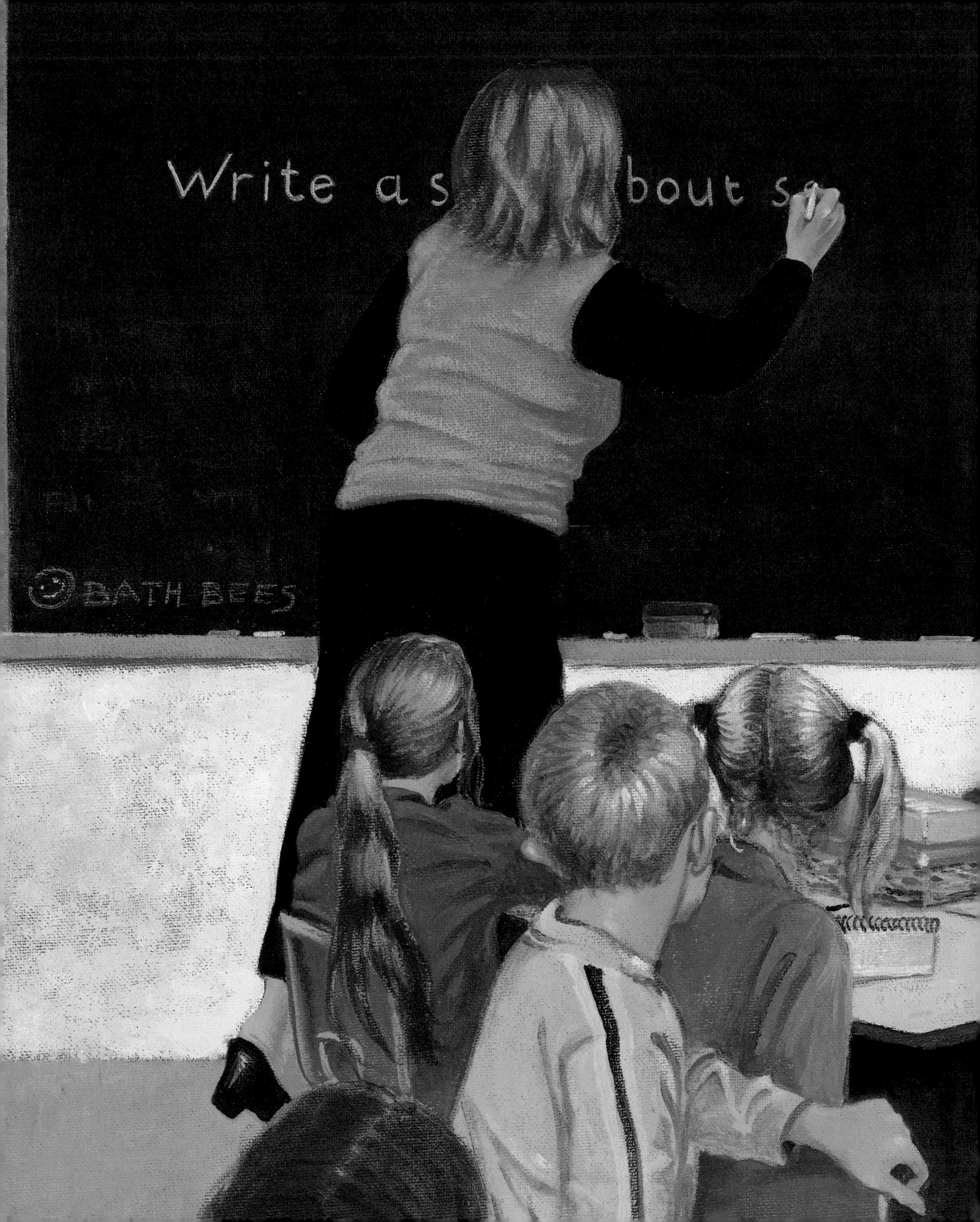
Write a s bout s
BATH BEES

I am in trouble. On Friday Mrs. Derksen gave our fourth grade class our first writing project. On the blackboard she wrote:

"Write a story about someone or something that has been very important in your life."

KEEP ON DRAWING

Now it's Saturday morning and my stomach feels nervous and my brain is going bonkers trying to come up with an idea.

I find Mom and Dad working in the garden. Mom is gathering herbs and Dad is nearby, fixing the crooked scarecrow.

I tell them about the project and my problem, but they're not much help.

"Go take a walk in the back," Dad says. "That always clears my mind."

"Write what you know," Mom suggests. "That always works for me."

So I decide to go for a walk. Our two big dogs, Buddy and Myles, nearly knock me over as they race down the lane. Mom's laugh fills the air.

As I wander down the trail and through the pasture,
I imagine what farms were like long ago.

Dad said that farmers used huge draft horses instead of tractors to
plow fields. It would be neat to have a horse that big! Big gardens
were planted to feed families all year round. There was no TV or
electricity or telephones. People used wood stoves for cooking
and staying warm. Nearly everyone drank warm milk, fresh from
the family cow. And it's hard to believe, but bathrooms were
stinky outhouses in the woods. Yuk!

Before there were farms, Dad said the land,
like much of Michigan, was mostly swamp-
land and woodland. Long before the farmers
moved here, the land belonged to the wilds.
Dad said even mammoths lived here!

Hmmm, what if mammoths aren't really
extinct at all but just really good at hiding?
I think I have even seen their footprints...

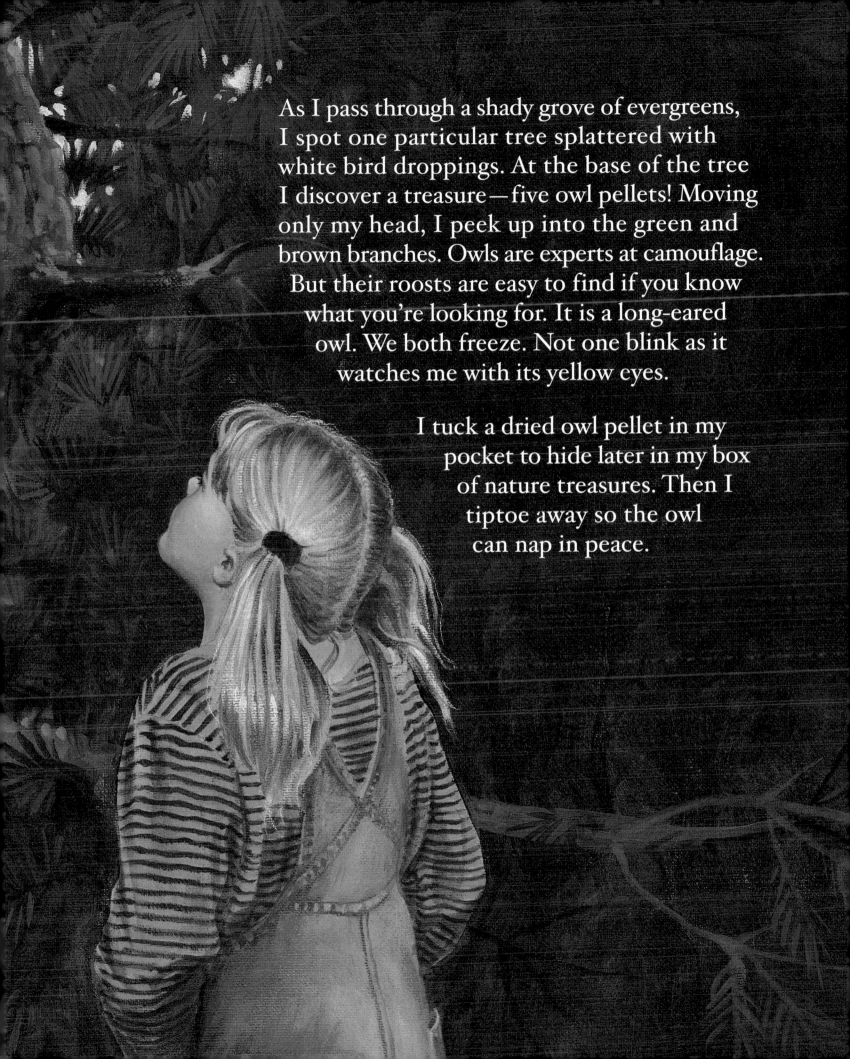

As I pass through a shady grove of evergreens, I spot one particular tree splattered with white bird droppings. At the base of the tree I discover a treasure—five owl pellets! Moving only my head, I peek up into the green and brown branches. Owls are experts at camouflage. But their roosts are easy to find if you know what you're looking for. It is a long-eared owl. We both freeze. Not one blink as it watches me with its yellow eyes.

I tuck a dried owl pellet in my pocket to hide later in my box of nature treasures. Then I tiptoe away so the owl can nap in peace.

As I walk out in the open field, I hear the screech of a hawk. A red-tailed hawk sails overhead in search of a midday meal. At the top of the ridge I spot sand piles from an empty fox den. I close my eyes and take a deep breath. A breeze carries the musky scent of fox to my nose.

The air is also filled with the smells of flowers and pine trees and sheep manure and fresh hay. Looking over the land, I realize just how much the farm has changed.

Over the years we have lived at Hazel Ridge Farm, Mom and Dad
have planted thousands of trees, dug five ponds, made wetlands,
and seeded wild prairies. They created an environment where all
of nature's creatures can feel safe. And I helped them.

Last spring, around this very spot, Dad and I planted a gazillion little pine trees. By the end of the day we were tired and dirty. I asked him what was so important about planting trees.

Dad looked around the property and said, "Trees provide food, shelter, and nesting areas for many wild creatures. As more houses are being built, natural areas are shrinking fast, and that means many plants and animals are losing their homes. We have to care enough about the land, Kelly, to restore and protect it. We can't do it all but we can at least start with our own back-yard." Mom and Dad feel it is everyone's responsibility to protect the land and share it with the wild creatures.

Then I asked, "Can I do more things to help?"

"The most important thing you can do, Kel, is to remember how we have protected and nurtured the land and share your stories with others."

Remembering is not such a hard job.

I look around and think about all the wild animals that share our farm. Springtime always means taking care of orphaned animals. There might be baby skunks and opossums in the kitchen, fawns sleeping in my old playpen, and lots of rowdy raccoons. We have shared our house with baby ducks, foxes, turkeys, and owls.

There are chores for everyone on the farm. My older sister and I use baby bottles filled with goat's milk to feed orphaned fawns. We take care of them until it is time for them to go back out into the wild. Sometimes we raise an orphan lamb and fawn together so they will keep each other company, just like sisters keep each other company.

A deer leaps from the tall grass but stops and looks my way. Maybe he was an orphan that stayed with us and now remembers me as a friend.

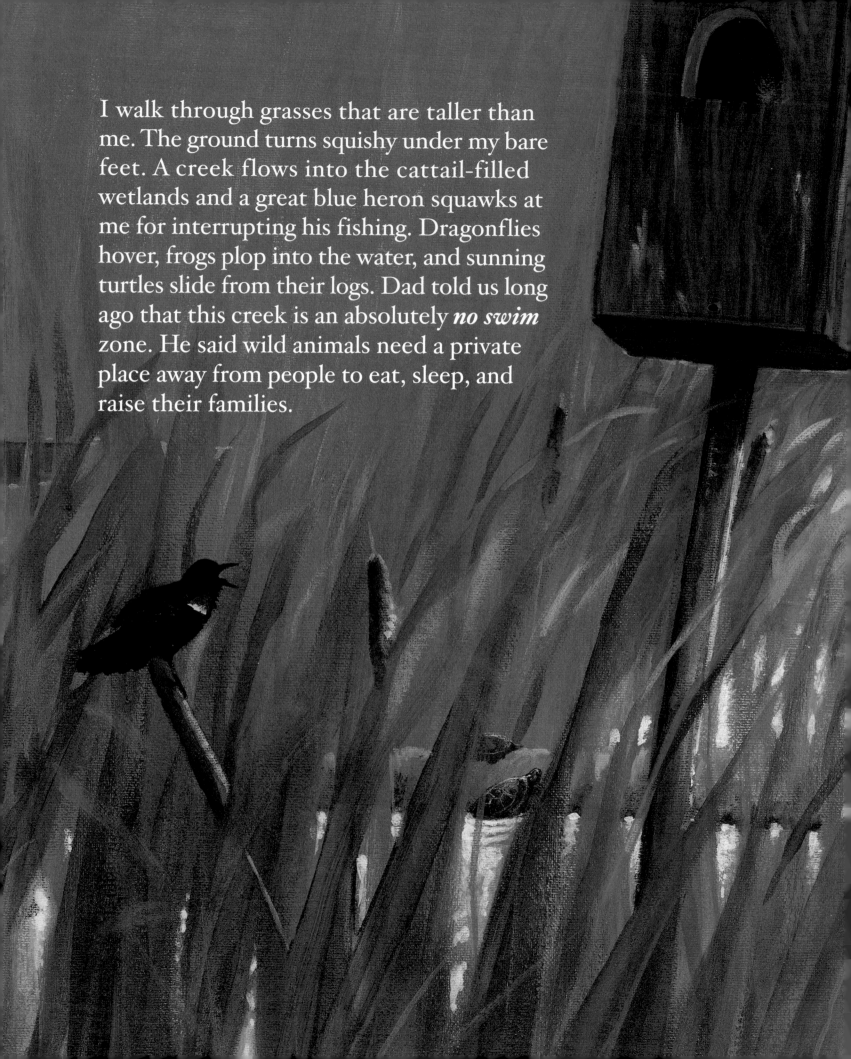

I walk through grasses that are taller than me. The ground turns squishy under my bare feet. A creek flows into the cattail-filled wetlands and a great blue heron squawks at me for interrupting his fishing. Dragonflies hover, frogs plop into the water, and sunning turtles slide from their logs. Dad told us long ago that this creek is an absolutely *no swim* zone. He said wild animals need a private place away from people to eat, sleep, and raise their families.

A kayak rests on the shore, nearly invisible in the tall grass. It was our birthday present to Dad last year. Now he can check for eggs inside the boxes we built for wood ducks.

I reach the prettiest spot on the farm. Last year Dad built a bench high in the branches of an old walnut tree. It takes nine steps up a ladder to reach the bench. I've climbed the ladder so many times I can do it with my eyes closed. Sitting on the bench, I feel like I'm in a big chair and I can see our whole farm from here.

When Mom and I walk the dogs after dinner, we usually end up at the tree bench. These are quiet times. Mom says the peace at the day's end warms her like a cup of chamomile tea.

Buddy and Myles charge past the walnut tree, yipping and howling, hot on a rabbit's trail. The rabbit finds safety in a thorny blackberry patch while the dogs circle the patch in frustration. I don't like thorny blackberry bushes.

Last summer I raced past Mom in the garden
and yelled, "Gonna pick berries! Love ya! Bye!"

There were so many berries everywhere I just kept
walking and picking and eating. I didn't really pay
attention to where I was going.

I got trapped in the sharp thorns of the thick bushes.
The more I struggled, the more tangled I became.
I tried to be brave but it was getting dark and cold.
I felt lost and alone. I cried but no one heard me.

Then suddenly Mom was there. She rocked me in her arms, whispering over and over again, "It's all right. It's all right."

We were both bleeding from our scratches and stained blue from the berries, but she held me until I stopped crying.

Mom hugged me tight as we headed for home. I told her how scared and lost I had felt. She squeezed my hand. "Kelly, every trail on this farm will lead you home. Some paths are longer and more challenging than others. As long as you remember the paths that lead you home, you will never be lost."

I hear the dinner bell clang and realize I have explored and daydreamed most of the day away. The bell means I have 20 minutes before dinner.

A narrow deer path is the quickest way
to my favorite spot so I imagine I am the
swiftest of all deer. As "Kelly the deer,"
I circle around the swamp, cut across
the fields, leap over fallen trees,
and duck under willow branches.

I reach my favorite spot on the farm...
we call it the cabin pond.

When I was three years old and my sister was five, Dad built a log cabin next to this pond. There are two sets of bunk beds, one bed for each of us. When the whole family sleeps there, Dad and my sister snore louder than four hibernating bears.

The cabin pond is also the swimming pond, but only the brave dare to jump in.

It looks cool and clear from above, but below in the murky bottom lurks Mr. Snapper. He is the most humongous snapping turtle in the world and can chomp off a toe with a single bite!

Dad promises us that turtles and fish stay far away from squealing girls so my sister and I always make lots of noise while we swim.

Many of the painted turtles living in our ponds came to us as "road saves." Dad always stops to pick up any turtles walking across the road and brings them back to our ponds. He hates seeing them smooshed by cars and he knows that they will be safe and happy in our ponds. We have tried saving turtles whose shells were cracked, but they never survive.

I hear the bell clang once more. Last call before dinner. The dogs jump the fence and beat me home. They know it's dinnertime, too.

At bedtime I pull out my nature treasure box from the bottom drawer of my desk to add today's owl pellet. In all, I have a snake's skin, a bird's nest, two fossil stones, leaves, a dead beetle, an empty eggshell, a plaster cast of a deer print that Dad showed me how to make, and a magic fairy wing.

The moon leaves shadows on my bedroom walls. When I was little I was afraid of the dark. I imagined the scariest monsters creeping outside my bedroom windows. One night Mom opened the windows as wide as they could go and hooted, "Hoo, hoo, hoo-hooooo." Jackson, the Great Horned Owl we had rescued, hooted back.

Mom cuddled with me in bed. "You never have to be afraid, Kelly, because Jackson will always be outside your window to protect you." I never felt afraid again.

Jackson hoots outside my window now to let me know he is there.

I hide away my treasure box. There's one last thing I want to do before I go to sleep and that is write today's adventures in my journal.

Sept. 23, Saturday night

I am so happy. This morning I was worried about what I was going to write for Mrs. Derksen's class but I found my story right in front of me! I spent the whole day exploring our farm. I think I know why Mom and Dad want to protect the farm. It's not just for the birds and plants and animals and stuff. They want to save it for me and my sister, too. It makes me realize how much I love my family, our farm, and all the animals that share this land. And that's a story worth writing about.

Good night, Jackson. Good night, Hazel Ridge.

"Hoo, hoo, hoo–hooooo"

Some of Nature's Treasures

Plaster cast of deer's footprint

Animal bones

Pine cone

Snake skin

Pheasant feather

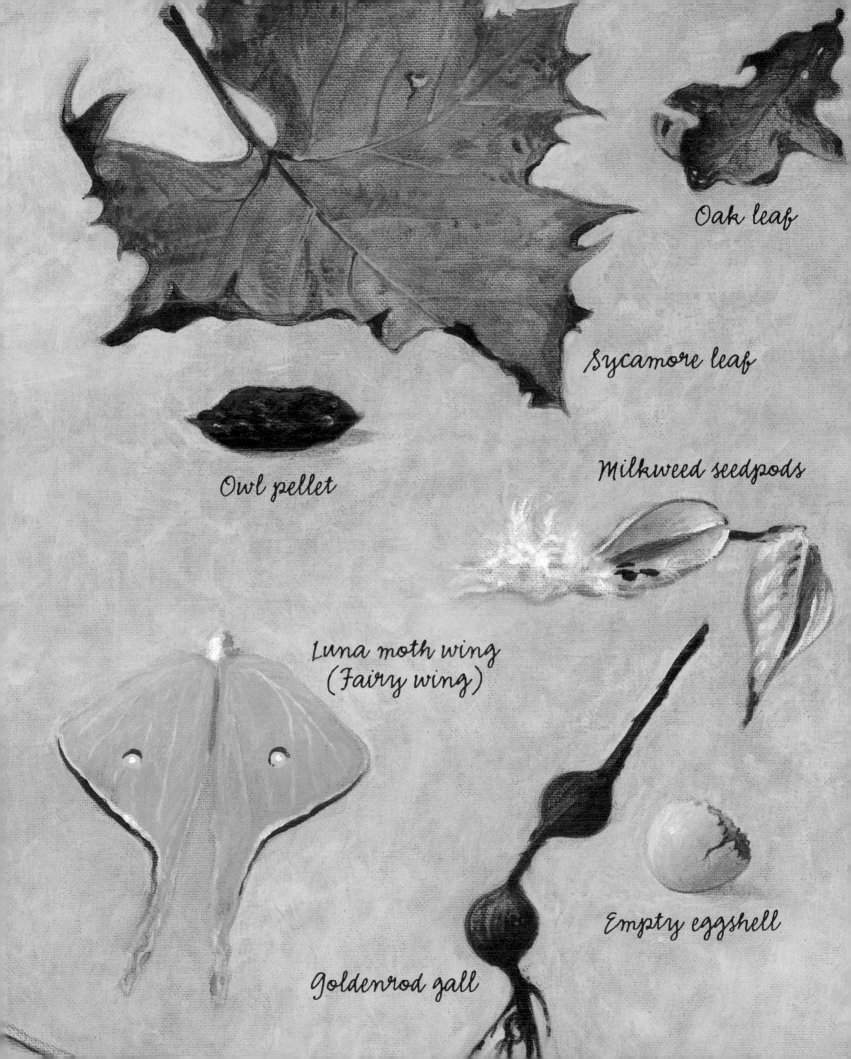

Oak leaf

Sycamore leaf

Owl pellet

Milkweed seedpods

Luna moth wing
(Fairy wing)

Empty eggshell

Goldenrod gall

How to Make Your Nature Treasure Box

Materials

1 shoe box (any size)
Construction paper (all colors)
Crayons or coloring pencils
Glue or tape

1. Cut construction paper to cover all sides and the lid of the shoe box.
2. Draw nature pictures on one side of each cut piece.
3. Glue or tape drawings on shoe box.
4. Let dry.
5. Fill box with nature items you find outside.

Some Neat Things to Put in a Nature Treasure Box

Different types of leaves
Dead bugs
Snake skins
Bird nests
Animal bones
Owl pellets
British soldier moss
Dried flowers
Plaster cast of an animal footprint

Fossils and arrowheads
Empty eggshells
Pheasant feathers
A map to your secret hiding place
Goldenrod gall
Seedpods
Cattails
Luna moth wing (fairy wing)
Pine cones

Some Helpful Tips About Your Nature Treasures

- Placing flowers and leaves in between coffee filters and then pressing them under a heavy book makes them look nicer and hold their shape better.
- Make sure all your animal bones are clean and dry.
- Only remove a bird's nest after its family has left for good. Winter is the best time because leaves have fallen and it's easier to spot the nests.
- Write your discoveries in a journal.